SHANAE STARNES

Win On Purpose

A Guide To Discovering Your Purpose In Life

This book was professionally typeset on Reedsy.
Find out more at reedsy.com

This book is dedicated to my beloved grandfather Thomas Jefferson Starnes who was affectionately known as "T.J". His actions of love and commitment for his family, community and business taught me that anything is possible. It has been 20 years since he departed this life but, he created a strong legacy that will live on for generations. I wish I could tell him that he continues to inspire me to win.

"I've learned that people will forget what you said, people will forget what you did, but people will never forget how you made them feel."

-MAYA ANGELOU

Contents

Preface

"Win On Purpose" is about my growth within myself. It took a long time to get here. But, I am here and I love it! To Win On Purpose means that I have to believe that I am a winner before I start the race.

In July, 2016 I, finally discovered my purpose in life. It was on the 19th of July blessed as always, it was a typical day. I felt a pressure in my chest that landed me in my doctor's office. What do you do when your heart is broken? I mean literally broken?

After depression settled and the realization that I had Congestive Heart Failure (CHF) I needed to get back up! I needed to get a plan in place so, I could begin to function again and not be silently depressed. With the help of my mother consistently checking on me. Not physically but mentally she reminded me that life is something to celebrate. I knew that regardless of the outcome of any situation, victory is based on an optimistic outlook.

The lesson I've learned and now share with you in this book is that our victories are about more than crossing the finish line first. It comes from making the most of the entire experience. Challenges are an opportunity for learning. Take time to assess weaknesses and work on turning them around by developing a strategy to avoid them in the future.

I continually strive to sharpen my skills and cultivate a positive attitude. Second chances are opportunities for self-improvement. I perform better each time I try again. I know I am a winner, even if I have to make multiple attempts. My place in the world is best served through ongoing self-development.

Today, I believe in myself and approach each race with confidence. I smile at the beginning because I am excited about the chance to learn something new. I smile at the end because I have embraced the experience.

I

Win On Purpose

1

Purpose For Your Life

Have you ever wondered whether finding meaning in life is actually important? Or is it just something made up by people?

Maybe you get the sense that you should be further along in life. Yet experience an overwhelming sense that you'll never get anywhere from where you are now.

If you've ever wondered whether personal development works, it does. To lead a content and successful life, it's imperative to find meaning in your life.

This is something that distinguishes you from others. The meaning you find in your life may not be the same as those around you. But that's fine. Your distinct meaning is what sets you apart.

Once you find the meaning in your life, you can become the best of your being. In addition to that, you will be able to polish your personality.

What Is Life Purpose?

Most people have no idea what they'd like to pursue or do with their lives. And this is not just high school graduates full of aspiring, wonderful dreams. In fact, it's most adults; even after finishing school, getting a job and making steady money. There's still room for clearly defining what their life purpose is.

In fact, it's a conflict that often begins in adult life. Seemingly simple questions like *"What do I want to do with my life?"*, *"What am I passionate about?"* and *"How can I make my life better?"* are all questions that pop into adult minds looking for ways to identify what they would like to do with their lives.

In other words, they still haven't been able to identify their life purpose. But is this really as complicated as it seems? Well, yes and no.

To put it simply, everyone exists on earth for an unspecified duration of time. People do different things during that time with some being important and others not so much. Among these things, it's the important things which give life its meaning and a sense of fulfillment. The unimportant ones are just a way to kill time.

To make matters a little more complicated, ignorance towards their true selves is something that most people live with for a long time. They set up their lives based on others' expectations and norms and in doing so may never be able to discover their true selves.

Others who set out on the path to self-discovery find out that the journey is neither easy nor pleasant. In fact, there are plenty of hurdles along the way. When you set out to find your life purpose, it means that you hold yourself, your set of beliefs and values and your likes and interests as top priority.

You look for things that make you truly happy, or rather fulfilled. This also means that on the way, you are going to displease others since you no longer want to live your life by their dictates.

Yes, this journey can include confusion, conflict, some fear, quite a bit of misunderstanding and a lot of doubt along the way. And last but not least, it'll also involve re-visiting many choices that you have made in life earlier. Think of it as spring cleaning of the mind that will ultimately lead you to your life's true purpose.

So What Is Life Purpose Really?

Life purpose is a lot of things, but foremost, it's the first step to living your life the *most conscious way*.

Here's one way to look at it- you may be very busy with a lot of chores and tasks every day. But if you don't have a purpose intended for those tasks, then every effort you make will mean very little in the end. So basically, the end goal may have nothing to do with your purpose.

This means that you could pursue you current goals for the next so many years and then come to realize that this wasn't what you wanted in the first place.

On the contrary, if you have a life purpose, then that's how you learn to lead a conscious life. Your efforts get directed towards something and you enjoy every minute of it. And although this doesn't imply that your problems disappear, at least now you know *why* you're trying to find a way around those problems.

You also know that you've discovered your life purpose when you feel energized in all your endeavors. You no longer dread the daily grind, but are eager to get your day started and get as much done as you possibly can.

How Do You Measure Life Purpose?

There can be a few determinants in this regard. For starters, there's making sacrifices. Achieving anything that's worth achieving involves sacrifices. Everything comes at a cost and very few things are uplifting or pleasurable all the time.

The question that arises here is what sacrifice or struggle are you ready to make or tolerate? If you find yourself giving in at the slightest chance of pressure, then obviously this choice isn't your life purpose.

But if you're willing to ride through the rough patches and stick with it no matter what, then you may be on to something. This is because what ultimately determines your ability to commit to something shows how much you care about that thing and how much it means to you.

For instance, if you wish to become a successful entrepreneur, but aren't good at handling failure, you won't get far. Or, say your dream is to become a professional artist, but don't like to see your work criticized or rejected, then there's not much scope for you out there.

But if the same purposes keep you going despite unpleasant experiences, staying awake long nights, or riding out the bad days, then you may just have discovered what you're really cut out for.

You can also determine if you've found your life purpose if you find sheer joy in doing something now that you also enjoyed doing as a child. Say you enjoyed writing as a child and only rediscovered the same joy of writing later on in life.

A lot of times people tend to lose touch with what they loved when they were younger. Oftentimes, it has a lot to do with the social pressure of adolescence or the professional pressure of young adulthood which wrings the passion right out of them.

Instead what remains behind is the lesson that the only reason to do anything is if there's a tangible reward for it. But if you can look beyond the physical reward for something and learn to enjoy the experience instead, it could be your true calling.

Vulnerability can also often point you in the direction of your real passion. If you're passionate about something, then you risk making mistakes to improve yourself.

Making mistakes leads to embarrassment and if becoming embarrassed stops you from doing something that you really want to do, then you should re-think your life purpose.

Your real life purpose won't let you care about getting embarrassed. It won't concern itself with what others think of you but urge you to pursue it instead.

When people feel like they've got no sense of direction or any purpose in life, it's because they don't know what's important to them. And when you don't know what's important to you, then you're just taking on other people's values and following their priorities instead of your own.

And this is exactly what this book aims to correct so that you can live your own life based on what's important to you, not what others think is good for you.

2

The Meaning Of Your Life

If you find meaning in your life, you'll be able to learn your purpose in this world. Experts believe that you can live your life in two ways. The first says that if you're conscious, you'll live along the same lines as others. Yet, you'll experience the same things differently.

The second way to live is to live unconsciously. Broadly speaking, if you live like that, life will just happen to you. Think of it as a giant wave that keeps pushing you forward. You have no control over where you're going or why you're going there. In fact the only thing certain about this situation is that you're just going with the flow. This kind of life isn't exactly ideal since you don't have much say in it. Yet, many of us live this way.

When you learn the meaning of life, you have a better sense of purpose. You tend to understand why you're in this world. Just like that, you will have a clearer view of how you can contribute to the world.

If you don't know your purpose, you'll hate getting out of bed. Your motivation to last through the week would be looking forward to the weekend. Put you in a challenging situation and you'll feel burnout even before trying. On the other hand, if you lead a meaningful life, you'll love the grind.

Here are some tips on why it's important to find meaning in life:

Gives Clarity and Focus

Look around yourself and you'll see so many people running after a host of popular things. Common offenders include earning more money, getting a house, and then getting an even bigger house. Goals also include getting a car, the latest technology and everything along those lines. Incidentally, all these are also material gains and rewards.

And while they may seem very important to you right now, do they really matter that much in the long run? How about looking for something that you're passionate about instead? Something that you thoroughly enjoy doing? Something that brings out the best in you?

It isn't uncommon that while running after money and luxuries, you become side-tracked from your real purpose. Finding your life purpose will help you become aware of things that are important.

Once you learn to look past these common needs, you'll see what's important. It'll help you set your goals and eliminate unimportant things from your life.

If you keep pursuing things you don't need, knowingly or unknowingly, you'll end up nowhere. By distinguishing between the important and unimportant, you won't feel lost and unaccomplished in 20 years' time.

You can also achieve success by finding the meaning in your life. Remember this one thing: Your success will be different from others. For you, success might be becoming the next Newton. For someone else, it might be owning the latest Audi.

But worry not. This is exactly what meaning brings in your life. Uniqueness and contentment. Every day, you have to become a better version of yourself. You have to get up and conquer the world. To achieve, succeed or excel, you have to first find the meaning in your life.

Teaches What Defines You

Have you ever felt that external factors are defining who you are? That you're being told what works for you instead of you figuring it out for yourself? Why does this happen? Probably because you don't have a life purpose or haven't figured it out yet.

When you lead a meaningless life, society starts to define you and the people around you shape you. If you keep living by others' definition of you, you'll find yourself in unfulfilling jobs and situations.

Being humans, we all need a means of sustenance. However, you may be stuck in a job that you hate. You needed a job so you got whatever was out there. The only reason you may have landed this job is because someone else recommended you for the position.

The result is that you end up going to your workplace tired and bored, surrounded by people you have nothing in common with, all because you had no direction in life- you just need a job.

But as soon as you find some life purpose, you can work towards a career that better fits your purpose. If you're leading a meaningful life, your means of sustenance can also become your passion. You can find yourself in a workplace that you enjoy and coworkers who are compatible with you. Once you have a meaning and a purpose, you'll clearly see the people you need. In addition, you'll also be able to cut out people who are toxic.

It's important to find compatibility in people and surround yourself with those who support your meaning. Being around like minded individuals who can help you become your best self can add even more to your life purpose.

Keeps You Connected With The Present

The more you engage in a purposeful life, the more it grows with you. At the same time it also makes you happier.

Remember how we talked about the important vs the unimportant? Well, a purposeful life will be no doubt very different from the pleasurable (unimportant) life that is transient, current and illusory.

In contrast, a meaningful life can become demanding and quite often a stressful one. More than worldly goods and luxuries, it requires planning, patience, ownership of actions, and the responsibility of the consequences of choices made. It's not as accommodating as a pleasurable life because purpose requires you to be patient, delay gratification and think for the long term.

When you do all this, it keeps you connected to the present. What this means is that you learn to live the best that you can in the present. Your purpose keeps you grounded to your present rather than postponing it into the future.

Say you're working on a book and need to get it done by a specific time. Now you also have a family, kids and other responsibilities to see. Your purpose, in this case is to get the book written so despite other commitments, you make your best effort to give time to your book.

At the end of the day, you'll know that you were able to squeeze time for what you love to do and fulfill your purpose, even though in a small way. It's one small step forward towards completing a project which means something to you.

A connection to the present also helps you stay more focused, passionate and gratified with what you have.

Focused, because you know how to stay away from distractions; Passionate, because it urges you on to reach your full potential; And Gratified, because you're living a value-based life.

3

Why Is It Difficult To Find Purpose In Life?

When you think about it, it seems easy enough to find yourself. However, once you've put this thought into action, things can quickly become hard.

When you are looking for meaning or purpose in your life, there are many obstacles that you face. This seemingly easy task can take quite a while for it to sort out. Here are some common issues that may be preventing you from discovering your life purpose:

Societal Influence

It's quite possible that you've already adopted the ways of society. Our society has certain standards through which we judge people and it's due to these standards why some people are "popular" while the others are not.

Perhaps societal influence is most impressionable in young adults. For example, if you're a high school student, you would see these factors around you. When you see that being a football player makes you popular, that's what you may want to be. Or you may want to be a cheerleader since they seem to be equally popular.

Once you see this, you strive for the purpose that has been set by people around you. All this might not appeal to you or it may not be your calling. However, you give in to the influence and ignore your route to self-discovery.

Say your purpose in life might be to be the next Steve Jobs. However, in an attempt to be as cool as the football player, you lose yourself behind.

And societal influence doesn't end here. In fact, for many it goes on beyond their adolescent years and pursues them even in their advanced years, always preventing them from finding their true calling.

Low Self-Esteem/ Self-Worth

This one's a real dilemma. How do you expect to love yourself if you've never been loved by others? Or you've never been told that you're worthy of it?

For many people, the road to self-discovery can be tough without self-love. If you've been criticized by everyone around you all your life, it can be hard for you to love yourself. It's possible that you've never been appreciated in your life for what you are. People around you may have always told you that someone else was better than you.

For instance, your parents may have always compared you with your cousins, friends or other peers. Your teachers may have told you how everyone else in the class was better than you. Or your boss has been quick to criticize your flaws but shown little or no appreciation for your work. This negative feedback can really stop you from being true to yourself.

In fact, it becomes harder to find your purpose until you love yourself unconditionally. Quite simply, how else will you learn about things you care about, or things that matter to you?

To find your purpose, you have to give time to yourself. If you don't consider yourself worthy of your own time and attention, you're in a bad place.

Because of all these factors, self-love becomes an impossible task. You constantly criticize your own self by comparing yourself to others. In addition to that, you don't think that you're good at anything.

Lack of Freedom to Dream

Not everyone gets to follow their dreams and it becomes one of the greatest factors stopping you from finding your purpose. Your purpose might lie in something that is considered 'unrealistic' by others.

Let's say you want to be a cosmetologist. Yet, everyone keeps telling you that it isn't a very "economic" decision.

They ask you how you'd feed your family. They also remind you of the increasing expenses and how your passion isn't going to be compatible with your finances. Even your parents have better options decided for you.

They tell you there are other lucrative jobs out there. If you want to do something unconventional, they will tell you 'it's impossible'.

With this constant discouragement to follow your dreams, you can't ever discover yourself. You lose the will to find what you were born to do.

Then there are certain things that you're required to do by a certain age. You're expected to get a degree by a certain age and then settle down. It all comes down to the societal norms once again. In a race to get a degree and start a career, you forget to listen to your calling. Your calling is the true you. It's something that makes you. Once you respond to that, you find your purpose. But if you're not given a chance to even think about following your dreams, how can you achieve them?

Fear of the Dark Side

Everyone has a dark side. People who come to terms with their dark side are the most successful ones. You can ignore this side of yours but you can't make it go away. Until you address it, this side will always remain.

As long as it's present, this side hinders you from discovering your purpose. The reason why you don't find your purpose is because you're scared to get in touch with this side. And you don't want others to see it either.

You think that if you keep hiding it, it will stop existing. But this isn't true. Your dark side is a portrait of your deficiencies. It represents your flaws and your failures. It encompasses the selfish and wrong desires that you have.

When you're on a journey of self-discovery, you'll have to encounter this side. Yet, the fear of this side keeps you from trying to find your purpose.

You fail to understand that this side can help you excel. Once you enlighten this side of yours, you can be your best self.

The problem is that you do not want those around you to see that you have this side. It is your little secret.

You're even afraid to see it yourself. How can you, a responsible father, have any selfish desire? How can you, a hardworking student, fail at being an honest person? You are too scared to face these questions.

Yet it all makes sense. You find solace in looking at the bright side of yourself. This is where your comfort zone lies. It's this side that makes you feel good about yourself. Despite that, this side will never help you find your ultimate purpose.

Another aspect of this dark side is a fear of questions you don't have answers to. It's easy and comfortable to be faced with questions that you have answers to but it's natural to feel hesitant facing questions you can't answer.

On the road to self-discovery, there are a lot of questions you can't always answer. The thought of facing these questions scares you and that's why you try to avoid them.

You become accustomed to easy knowledge that you have of yourself. And because of this, you don't want to be in an ambiguous situation. *"How can I not know this about myself?"* This is what stops you from finding your purpose.

So, if you somehow manage to cross all these obstacles, you can find your purpose. It's just a constant battle with yourself and your deepest fears. If you win it, you're golden.

4

The Difference Between Happiness and Fulfillment

Happiness is a code that all humans have. It's deemed essential and everyone seems to believe it. In fact, it's gained a religion-like reverence that everyone follows. But happiness is something that is relatively subjective. It can be big, small, long term or short term. And since it's more of a general term, everyone can relate to it. Some common things that make everyone happy are family, career, a good job and money.

Fulfillment on the other hand is something more personal. It's yours. And as such, fulfillment for everyone is different. You can experience fulfillment when you pursue something you're passionate about, such as a goal or a dream. Perhaps you're all about helping others such as volunteering or maybe you're that person who engages in activities promoting continuous growth and learning. If you compare the two, you'll notice that fulfillment has a much deeper and longer lasting effect than happiness. Fulfillment is what you need to strive for.

Why? Here's why:

Fulfillment is Unique to You

The foremost reason why you should opt for fulfillment is that it's something unique to you. It's something that sets you apart from others around you.

Maybe eating right and exercising is what fulfills you as you know you're doing something right to improve your overall health. Your friend, on the other hand may find workouts not so fulfilling as better health may not be what they are looking for. To them, your workout sessions together may just be a drag.

So while happiness is something that everyone feels the same way about, fulfillment will give you a unique sense of being and purpose. In fact, unlike happiness which is strictly a feeling, fulfillment is something that you attain by investing time and effort. It's a feeling of hard work and dedication that leads to the accomplishment of your goals. In its own way, fulfillment makes you a complete person.

In terms of their time spans, happiness is a fleeting, short term sensation while fulfillment is eternal. Being short-term, happiness isn't realistically sustainable. After all, how many people do you know who are actually happy all the time? Probably not that many.

But when you compare it to fulfillment, you may know quite a few who are very, very content with what they have achieved. This is because the idea of fulfillment makes it okay to not be happy all the time. It tells you that things will be okay even if you're going through a rough patch.

Fulfillment gets etched in your brain and remains with you for a very long time. For example, you do something such as blogging which gives you a feeling of fulfillment.

If being a lifestyle blogger makes you feel fulfilled, you'll invest all your creativity and energy into being one.

Along the way, you'll surely have some bad days. Everyone does. Yet, you'll always have the contentment in your heart that you are doing something purposeful.

With happiness, you never know how long you're going to be happy for. If you're happy now, you could hear some upsetting news, making happiness dissipate quickly. Happiness is not as personal since anything can take it away from you in a matter of seconds.

Opposed to that, fulfillment is not affected by incidents, feelings or people. It belongs to you. It is yours and you can keep it for as long as you want. Nothing and no one can steal your sense of fulfillment from you.

Fulfillment Gives Meaning To Success

Being happy with your success is great. However, this feeling will eventually go away. You might've won an Oscar and felt like you're on top of the world at that moment. However, if it's not something that fulfills you, that award is just a miniature statue in your home. On the contrary, if something makes you feel fulfilled, it gives you joy every day.

Happiness is simply not sustainable. Fulfillment is. This is why that's what you should aim for. If you aim towards fulfillment, you're bound to work hard. If all you want to be is happy, you don't need to do much. Even being with your favorite person can make you happy.

Just like that, listening to any song can make you happy. If you are a foodie, a doughnut can brighten up your day. Sometimes, happiness can make you lazy too. Hanging out with someone you like will make you happy. However, it will distract you from things that you are supposed to do.

When you strive for fulfillment, you will get things done on time. You will suddenly get an urge to get things done. At the end of the day, when everything is done, you'll feel complete. You'll be content knowing that you made something out of your day. Staying in your comfort zone makes you happy but it won't take you anywhere.

To be happy, you can take shortcuts but you can't do that with fulfillment. This is why you will go the extra mile to be fulfilled. Plus, if you're doing something that fulfills you, you'll also be more willing to try new things. You'll think of all the ways you can get better at it.

Suppose your job is fulfilling for you. Now, you won't dread the weekdays. You may even think of your work even during the weekends. This probably explains really well why some people are always immersed in their work. It only happens when you find fulfillment in your work. It makes you content and your life peaceful.

Happiness is Just One Feeling

Happiness is a single feeling. Think of it like a rainbow. It's just one color. On the other hand, fulfillment is made up of so many colors. It is made up of passion, drive, emotion, grieve and failure.

You have to go through all that to feel fulfilled. This is what makes fulfillment so special. There is nothing wrong with looking for happiness. But do you want to miss all the colors of the rainbow for just one color?

There are times when you are not exactly happy but you are fulfilled. For example, if you are working for long hours as a doctor, you may not be happy. You may have seen some painful cases throughout the day. You may have even cried when you're a procedure didn't go as planned. It could be a day filled with grief, misery and hard work.

Yet, at the end of the day, you feel peace at heart. This is because you feel fulfilled. You know that you did something which completes you. It's your purpose in this world and you do it religiously.

For most, this feeling is enough to keep them going. Even when you may not be happy, the feeling of fulfillment drives you on. When you are fulfilled, you always look for ways to get better.

You must remember that happiness is an important element of life too. However, you can only be truly happy if you live a fulfilling life.

5

Beware Of False Purpose

I f you look around yourself, you'll see that most people follow the same dream. So much so that they all seem to have the same purpose. The most common example of this is how everyone believes their purpose in life is to earn money. In addition to that, starting a family also accompanies this desire to acquire wealth.

This will sound very familiar to most people only because these are the words of your parents, teachers and friends. You've always heard people talk about these basic things. They're repeated so often that it seems like these things are the sole purpose of humanity.

But do you ever think about what role you had in determining these purposes for yourself? Were you ever consulted in establishing these goals or are they mere echoes of others telling you what your goals should be?

Chances are that somewhere along the line others did the deciding and determining for you. Your elders, mentors, coaches and teachers took it upon themselves to decide for you without including you in the decision making process.

So what you thought was a choice was nothing more than suggestions or conditioned messages letting you believe that you were the one making the choices. Yet, at best they were instructions that you were asked to follow to determine the course of your life.

But if you think about it, there's something that just doesn't add up as these are purposes imposed on you by others.

It can be very easy to believe that a false purpose is your actual purpose in life. You could be influenced by family, colleagues and society. All these factors sometimes convince you that a certain purpose is your true one. However, in reality, it may not be so at all.

Recognizing False Purpose

The easiest way to recognize false purpose is that it's not your calling. Most often, it's something that has been imposed upon you by people. It could be a thought, an idea or a suggestion. But it's not your thought or idea.

Many life coaches talk about how finding your purpose isn't related to money or career. It's about finding your true self. This is the self that you've hidden underneath the needs of people around you.

It's quite true that you tend to hide your real purpose underneath people's needs. The society needs you to be a busy, nine-to-five person. So, you hide the carefree artist inside you.

Your parents need you to get a good degree. So, you curb your desire to sing and dance for a living. Your family needs you to be there at all times. So, you hide your desire to be a tour guide.

It's due to all these reasons that you adopt a false purpose. Don't be fooled by this purpose. It doesn't come from within you. It's being fed to you by others.

Suppose you're watching a movie with friends. You want to watch an adventure movie but they are more inclined towards a comedy. You may resist for a while but will eventually give in to their consistent nagging.

In the bigger picture, this is how people around you can manipulate you into believing that the false purpose is your calling.

Why You Need to Steer Clear of False Purpose

Now that you have an idea of what a false purpose is, you need to steer clear of it. Your false purpose can destroy you. It can make you do things that you don't enjoy or find meaning in.

At some point in life, maybe ten years from now, you'll regret not only the purpose but also the time you spent aiming for it. If you run after a false purpose, you'll realize it sooner or later. In the beginning, it may seem like you are doing things right.

Then you look around you and comfort yourself by saying that everyone else is doing the same thing too. Yet, deep inside, you lack both contentment and happiness. Then, you have an epiphany. A time when everything comes crashing down. You realize how you are just like others.

You think to yourself, *"What have I done that they haven't?"* *"How am I different from them?", "How is my life more fulfilling than theirs?", "Did I spend my youth, grinding and working, to be just like others?"* If you steer clear of such false purposes, only then do you find meaning in your life. To do so, you have to listen to yourself. What is your being saying to you?

Don't listen to others around you. Don't listen to the guy telling you to be an engineer just because he knows someone who is successful as one. Your true purpose is something you want. It is something that you have thought for yourself. You're not expected to do it. You just want to.

That is the beauty of a true person. You won't have to drag yourself to fulfill this purpose. Instead, you'll just get the energy for it naturally. Your passion will drive you to do your best.

Also, when you steer clear of false purpose, you do everything fearlessly. When you're forced into a false purpose, it is often due to fear. The fear of your parents or the fear of being rejected by the society.

However, when you find you true purpose, you do it with love. There's no fear of letting anyone down. You know you're doing this for yourself.

How Can You Steer Clear of False Purpose?

If you want to steer clear of false purpose, you need to listen to yourself only. Ignore what everyone else has to say. Spend time with yourself and learn about yourself. You'll find what drives you. If you care enough for yourself, you'll find the things that excite you. The most important thing is not to be fearful.

Don't fear failure but be ready to face it. Don't fear rejection but have the guts to face it. People might tell you that you have disappointed them. But it doesn't matter.

You might be wondering, *"How do I know I am not pursuing a false purpose?"* The best way to find this is by seeing if what you are doing makes you feel fulfilled.

If you're following your true purpose, you'll feel inspired by it every day. You'll find new things in it to love every day. On the other hand, a false purpose will show its flaws very soon.

To steer clear of this flawed purpose, you need to define your purpose. If you have defined your purpose well in advance, you won't have any regrets later.

Defining your purpose will give you a clear indication about your next move. This will ensure that you aren't going towards the pursuit of false purpose.

What matters is you and your ultimate fulfillment. Don't let anyone tell you that you disappointed them because you didn't go into medicine just like the rest of your family. If making music is your purpose, do that.

Let go of all the pretending, the core of your true self is waiting. The philosophy behind this concept is to let yourself in. Once you allow that to happen, you won't even need to find yourself. Your true self will just appear in front of you. This is the ultimate way to find your true purpose.

Just be yourself and do your thing. You're not everyone else around you so don't even try to be them.

6

Define Your Purpose

Finding your life's purpose can help you reach great heights. Before you find your purpose, you need to define it. It's only logical that you do everything in steps.

Whenever you decide to do anything in life, you take a step-wise approach. From performing reactions in a lab to cooking, everything needs to be done in steps. So, it is quite logical to define your purpose before you set out to find it. Before you serve the world, you need to define this place. You can't get to this place until you have first defined it.

Gives You Direction

Defining your purpose gives you a definite direction. It directs you towards your ultimate goal in life. If you want to achieve something in life, you have to be clear about your purpose. The most successful people will tell you that you need to have a definite purpose to win. Plus you must also have a strong desire to achieve this purpose.

If you have no direction, you'll end up going around in circles. Think of it as a journey. If you are going somewhere, not only do you need directions but also a destination to reach. But you'll never reach there if you don't have the directions. Similarly, if you have no definition, you can't get to your purpose. When you define your purpose, you know exactly what you're aiming for.

Defining your purpose is the best way to dig deep in yourself. You need to ask yourself why you are doing something or why you need to do it. But no one said it would be easy. When you first start the process, you're bound to be confused. There will be so many questions that you can't answer and you'll face ambiguities about yourself.

However, as soon as you define your purpose, all these doubts and confusions go away. You're able to see your goals clearly and will know how to reach those goals. People who are successful know what they want and why they want it. They have a sense of direction. Most importantly, they know what success means. They're aware of why they need to be successful or lead a meaningful life.

Once you define your purpose, everything you do will be in consistency with your goals. Every action of yours will get you closer to your aims and purpose. The first step is always to know "Why?" Defining your purpose will help you filter out your actions. You'll be able to prioritize the things that you need to do. In the same way, you'll also learn about the things you need to cut out.

Keeps You from Getting Distracted

Defining your purpose also keeps you from getting distracted. When you're on a quest to find your purpose, you'll be side tracked by a lot of things. To prevent this from happening, it's important to have a clear sense of where you're going. If you just wake up one day and decide to do something, you won't be very successful.

On the contrary, planning and defining will get you wherever you want. If you have a well-defined purpose, you'll actually live life and not just survive. For example, you might believe that your purpose in life is to serve others. Unless you know how you can do it, you can't do it. You might get distracted by people around you. They may tell you that you can do so by being a doctor or a teacher.

So if your purpose isn't defined, you get distracted by other peoples' suggestions. And you set upon a path that's not compatible with your calling. But if you define your purpose, you find the right path. You need to ask yourself important questions such as why you want to serve others? What drives you to do so? Why it is that this is your purpose and not something else?

After answering all these questions, you'll have a better sense of your purpose. Just like that, you'll clearly see the path you need to take. When you have defined your purpose, you're not afraid to take risks. You're not afraid of doing new or unconventional things. This definition will set the principle for your journey.

Keeps you Organized

When your purpose is well-defined, you remain organized. Instead of constantly thinking of what you need to do next, you already have a plan set out. But when you do not have a definition in your life, you're always busy thinking. The process of thought is time-consuming and if you get stuck in this process, you can't hope to go beyond.

To define your purpose, you have to give time to the thinking process. When you're done with it, you know exactly what needs to be done. You can enlist all the things that you need to do. If you've defined your purpose well, you can make a day-to-day plan. Some people are lucky in this regard as they have those "aha" moments which enlighten them.

Others have to think for a while. Some may even have to look around for inspiration. As soon as you have found your inspiration and your definition, you can start your journey. Think of it as a car ride. To start the ride, you need a car first. Then, you need to have a clear idea of where you're going and why you're going there. If you don't know these things, you'll never be able to start.

But if your thoughts are well-organized, you won't have any doubts or confusion. Nothing will be able to distract you. Organization is what you do before you do something so things don't get mixed up.

This makes a lot of sense. If all your thoughts and plans are mixed up, you're in trouble. Define your purpose. Stick to a single plan and you'll eventually find your purpose.

Gives You Time for Experimentation

While you're defining your purpose, it gives you a chance to experiment. This is the time when you can explore yourself. When you're defining yourself, you'll be able to see your real self. If you simply set out to find your purpose, you might find something completely different along the way. It might be something that will completely change your purpose. Then, all your previous effort will go to waste.

Now, consider this. If you've already done all the defining, exploring and experimenting, you will be more certain. By experimenting, you learn about yourself. You see your passion, your interests and your talents. When you define your purpose, you may find things that surprise you.

Imagine yourself as a video game character. You have to read the instructions first or watch a tutorial video. Without that, you'd be completely lost. Just like that, you need to define your purpose. Look within to find your drive, your reason and your calling.

7

Purpose And Passion Is Personal

You may have all the prerequisites for happiness including a job, a happy family and a big house. But why is it that you don't feel fulfilled? If you constantly feel that something is missing, then the missing piece of the puzzle could be your purpose.

At this stage, you need to sit down and re-evaluate your life. Only by asking yourself and looking into your self will you find the answers. No one knows you better than yourself. So, it's you and only you who can find your purpose.

Your job is to find this purpose and polish it well. Because when you accomplish that, your life becomes so much more meaningful.

Find What Excites You

Most of the time, your purpose is what excites you. If you current job doesn't excite you, it's definitely not your passion. Do you have to drag yourself out of bed every day? Are you constantly looking at the clock during work?

All of us are born with a talent. We all have something inside us that makes us different and special. You just need to find this thing. Just a little warning: You won't be perfect at it the first time. You can't really expect to be perfect at something even if it's your talent. You have to learn it, earn it. Even the best of artists and musicians have to practice and learn.

But then how do you know what your talent is? It's something that comes easy to you. It could be drawing. If you enjoy practicing your craft with a pen or pencil, love to learn more about art, admire great artworks and look up to fine artists, then being in a creative and artistic field could be your true calling.

If it's always been easier for you to draw than read or write, then look that way. Maybe you could draw straight lines and perfect circles without any tools, and your notes had more doodles than writing on them. Clues like these tell you where you real passion lies and you shouldn't hesitate to answer that call.

Here's something- have you ever had that feeling when you do something for the first time but feel like you already know how to do it? That is the feeling you need to look for.

You have to trust in something in your life. It could be "gut, destiny, life, the karma, whatever. This approach may make a difference in your life.

Ask Yourself Why

'Why' is one of the most powerful questions ever asked. You need to ask yourself why you want to do a certain thing. Or why not? It's important to focus on the clarity of purpose. If you know the why behind the things you do, you will find your purpose easily.

As an example, consider the whys associated with your job - Maybe you're doing this job because it earns you a fine living. Maybe you're in this career because your parents pressured you. Or, you could be doing something just because all your friends were.

If these reasons justify your whys, then you're not doing what your purpose in life is. When you ask yourself 'Why' and the answer should be fulfillment. And that's when know you're face to face with your purpose.

You need to ask yourself "Why do I want to draw?". If the voice from inside tells you that it's to get meaning and fulfillment, then you're on the right path. This path will take you to your propose. If the voice inside you tells that you are doing something out of fear or to "fit in", then you need to let go immediately, for that isn't your purpose.

Once you figure out the why, follow Nike's motto and Just Do It. Because the more you act, the more things become clearer. So instead of overthinking whether something will work out or not, should you try it or what if you don't make money at it, start taking small steps towards your calling.

On the way there will always people around you who will have discouraging words for you. They'll tell you that your career path is unrealistic and useless. Or, there are those who will forcefully make you believe that something else is your pursuit. You have to ignore all these voices and listen to yourself instead.

Your true passion lies only in the things that you enjoy and love. Don't let others dictate this to you or allow anyone to tell you that your passion is useless. Since it's something that defines you as a person, you shouldn't care about others' opinions or expectations. Just remember that you're doing it for yourself. Because you owe it to yourself.

Explore Your Options

Many people also get stuck because they try to find the ONE thing that they're meant to do. But in doing so, you may waste your time looking for the wrong thing, actually find something and then realize that it's not for you, or just become disheartened when that something doesn't work out for you.

But why limit yourself to this ONE mentality when you could do so much more? The idea that you have only one thing that's meant for you can limit you from fulfilling your potential. For instance, you may be a life coach, who writes, travels, speaks, teaches, mentors and designs at the same time. You may enjoy every aspect of this job, being equally good at all of them. You may feel equally passionate about being in any of these roles which makes the whole experience of being a life coach more meaningful.

So stop thinking that there's only one singular purpose for you when you could be doing so much more with passion. So don't hesitate to jump in and try new things. Stop trying to resist the unknown for maybe that's where your calling is hiding.

Do follow your passions to make your life more purposeful, for when you live a passionate life, it becomes your purpose as well. In fact, you only need to look for a purpose when passion is lacking from your life. This makes you feel disconnected from life so to fix this void, simply add in more passion. If you need help with that, look at people who inspire you for they can help you find your passion.

For instance, if an artist or a designer inspires you, their field could be your passion too. Do you find yourself spending all your time on social media pages of fashion bloggers or designers?

Don't Suppress Your Doubts

Suppressing your doubts is something that can stop you from finding your purpose. By definition, doubt is a feeling you get when you have to do something, but there's more than one course of action to choose from. You're not sure which option you should pick, so you give in to doubt.

Although doubt always involves uncertainty about which decision will turn out best, it's not actually a bad thing to experience. If you let your doubts surface and come to terms with them, you're still making progress. But if you keep ignoring them, your life will become a mess.

For example, do you have doubts about your current job? Do you feel like you could be much better at something else? Give this thought time and find what you are better at. Even when you do think you have found a purpose and you have doubt, let that come to surface too. Otherwise, you'll be stuck with a false purpose.

In finding your purpose, you'll have doubts, fear and ambiguities. Always remember the final point and the joy you get once you are there. With this thought in mind, you will definitely discover your purpose.

8

A Purposed Filled Future

The grind doesn't end once you discover your purpose. When you finally know what gives your life meaning, you are excited, pumped and passionate. But, is that enough? Well, actually no. It's not.

The next step in the process is to transition to your life purpose. This means making changes, perhaps lots of changes. So how do you transition? Here's how:

Set Your Goals

After finding your purpose, you have to set your goals. If there are no goals or aims, your purpose is useless. It's just an ideology that is not being put into action. You have to give life to this purpose. The transition state is the state where you start to give life to your purpose. This is when you need to plan how you're going to show your purpose to others.

No one can go back and make a brand new start but, anyone can start from now a make a brand new ending. In your transition phase, you learn how to make your awesome ending.

For example, you have discovered that your purpose is to blog and inspire others. What are you going to inspire others about? Are you going to start a self-help blog? Is your aim to be a fashion inspiration for others?

You can't just get a website and wait for things to happen. Instead, you need to start writing. Put on your working pants and get to work. You can't be a successful writer with just an idea in your head. What you need to do is to put this idea on paper.

Likewise, you can't transition to your life purpose without a vision. If you don't have a vision, there's no way you can succeed. Your vision is what defines your purpose. If you have a well-defined goal and your purpose is clear to you too, the journey becomes way easier. Without a goal, you are just wandering around aimlessly. You'll lose your purpose, your drive and ultimately, your dreams.

This is exactly how you need to transition to your purpose. Tell yourself that getting ten thousand readers on your blog will be your reward if you work hard. This will keep you motivated to transition to your purpose.

You might not achieve what you wanted but it's fine. At least, you've started the transitioning process. You'll get there sooner or later.

The Fear Factor

The major reason why most people fail to transition to their purpose is fear. The fear of disappointing yourself and those around you. Or the fear of not being good enough. There are these questions hanging like swords over your head. Will my passion make me a living? Am I really as good as I thought? Will I disappoint my family, friends and myself if I pursue my higher purpose? Will it matter?

However, you shouldn't let the fear of judgment, rejection or disliking stop you from being your true self. How true is that? Aren't these all the factors that stop you from being who you are?

Things will be hard. When you are transitioning to your purpose, things won't always be easy. There will be times when you may want to go back to your previous, miserable, meaningless life, or your comfort zone. In these times, you have to remind yourself why you started in the first place.

If things were going to be easy, then everyone would be doing it. What's the point of anything if it's unbelievable easy? The fear of change stops you from transition to your purpose. The fear of leaving your old life behind pushes you away from your purpose. There are so many people who have their purpose in front of their eyes. Yet, they are too scared to hold it or get it.

Remind yourself why you took the first step. That will keep you going. It'll be hard to steer clear of people who divert you from your purpose. These are the people who have always been around you. Ignoring them will take a while and some effort.

Similarly, fear of deteriorating relationships stops the transition process. What you need to remember is that anyone who is sincere to you will support you. Once you let go of all your fears, transition becomes really easy.

You realize that there's nothing holding you back from achieving your purpose. Your current reality has formed a comfort zone around you. This is exactly what you need to get out of. You can only transition to your purpose once you leave your comfort zone.

How to Make This Transition

This is the big question. Finding your purpose seems like an easier task compared to this. When you're trying to find your purpose, you are just looking into yourself. You're finding what you need to do in life.

However, the transition phase requires action. It requires you to do something more than just contemplating. Financials are very important. Part of the reason why most people do not go for their dream job is that their dream job does not earn them enough.

If you want to transition to your true purpose, you need to have a financial purpose. Your blog won't start earning your immediately. So, how are you going to eat and live for the time that your passion is not earning you? This is what you need to plan before your transition to your purpose.

You can start in steps. Get a part time job that runs the house. Now, you can spend rest of the time on making your blog a success. Or you can keep your blog running with your current job.

You can always leave your current job once the blog is earning you enough. It will be hard to balance the two. But isn't that what following your purpose is all about? A few extra hours will make you feel more fulfilled than that nine-to-five work.

Systems Are Important

To transition to your life purpose, you need to have a system in place. If blogging is your purpose, you need to have websites and photo editors. You need to get in touch with other people from the field to guide you.

Look around and find people like you. Socialize with them and make your own little family. This family supports your purpose and will help you transition to it.

Your blog isn't enough. Head over to social media and increase your presence there too. Get in touch with people and let them know about you. Part of the transition process is to make others aware of your purpose.

Isn't this what musicians, painters, authors, scientists and artists do? They don't hide away their purpose. They bring it out to the world. Letting the world experience your art, music, inventions and words is the best way to transition.

Slowly yet eventually, you will get there. The transition process is just as fulfilling as the final result. Give it your undivided time and attention.

Your Next Steps

Living purposefully is one of the most, if not the most enjoyable experience you can have in life. You know that when you live with a purpose life just flows. On the way, you're able to carve your own way as you pass through the ups and down, with your purpose always holding you strong.

This is the life you want to live. This is the purpose you want to follow and these are the benefits you want to enjoy. A purposeful life is a meaningful life worth living.

9

8 Ways To Win On Purpose

1. Make Your Goals Measurable And With A Timeline.

Once you've identified your personal feelings, and you have your general goals set, we're going to tighten everything up and make it all super-specific.

There are two ways you can do this, depending on what the goal is.
A) Super-specific outcome goals.

These goals tend to be more popular with people. They're goals where you have
very tightly defined aims and deadlines, such as:
- Be earning $5k in passive income every month by next year
- Sign up ten clients in 60 days
- Make $1000 with my new Kindle book
- Lose 10 pounds in 45 days
- These goals add a little more pressure on you.

You might use them in a back-against-the-wall situation, where you need to earn a degree of money in a time or fit into a dress by your high school reunion. The disadvantage to this type of goal is that it often puts people in a "take every possible action and see what sticks" mindset, versus making long-term, lasting change.

Also, the goals are often arbitrary numbers. And if they're not reached, people feel like failures - no matter how hard they worked or if external circumstances got in their way. For example, you might have a goal to earn $5k in a month, but then a death in the family derails you for a week. Or maybe you have a goal to lose 10 pounds, but no matter how hard you work, your body just won't release the weight.

The best way to use this type of goal is if you have plenty of time to create great habits AND course correct if things aren't working. For example, if you want to be making $5k a month by a year from now, you can spend most of the time building up the right habits for yourself. But if you find yourself in month 6 and you aren't where you planned you'd be (which we'll cover more in-depth later on in this guide), you can course correct and try something else.

B) "Take-the-right-action" goals.

These are goals where you're taking steps to get to where you ultimately desire to be. For example:
- Eat greens with at least 50 meals this month
- Drink 80 oz of water each day
- Write two books in a year
- Go for a walk three times a week

When to make these kinds of goals: These are the goals to concentrate on when you want to build up healthy habits. For example, let's say you want to feel healthier. We all know that when you make sure you get in enough greens and water, you start becoming healthier. And so creating goals around getting more of both on a constant basis helps ensure you feel better.

These are goals that are a bit more spacious. You're trusting that the right habits will create results over time, and so you're making lifestyle goals instead of short-term crash diet plans such as "lose 10 pounds in a month."

I prefer these types of goals most of the time. Building up the right kinds of habits gives you a long-term edge and creates a more solid foundation for who you want to become.

Before you move on from this section, choose a goal or two from your list if you haven't already, and set clear timelines as appropriate. Ensure you've worded your goals, so they are distinct and MEASURABLE. I want you to know exactly what you're working towards and the timeline in which you're going to be doing it.

Remember this isn't about setting your deadlines in stone, but rather about being specific. You'll be able to course correct if you find you are not making the progress you'd like. Choose a timeline that feels like a stretch, but you know it can happen. Creating $500k or losing 100 pounds in a month is tough. Sure, there might be exceptions like winning the lottery or getting some surgery, but for most people, it's not going to happen. With those goals, you'd be best off choosing a year timeline.

When in doubt as you create a super-specific goal, give yourself a little more time - especially if you're embarking on something new. You can always make the goals happen faster. For now, pick your targets and deadlines and have them ready to work with as we continue with this process.

Don't worry about the HOW you're going to make anything happen just yet. That's coming next. In fact, we're going to go over an example using all the steps right now.

EXAMPLE

Step #1: Earn $5000 a Month.

You knew that you wanted to be earning $5k a month by this time next year. That's great! Now we can move onto the next step:

Step #2: Brainstorm how you can get there.

Here's where we're going to ask ourselves, "How can I make this happen?" Your mind is a brilliant thing. And when you ask it the right questions, you'll be amazed at the answers you can come up with. Here's where you're going to be very creative. List out all the ways that you can make your $5k/month goal happen (or whatever your goal is).

Don't censor yourself. Just let it all out, no matter how crazy or wild your ideas seem. If you're too busy judging your thoughts, you'll block your creativity. Write out for a solid 5-20 minutes and come up with at least 15 different ideas.

For the $5k example, some ideas of things you might find:
- Have a membership website where 250 people pay me $20 a month
- Have five people pay me $1,000 a month for coaching
- Create a $50 product and sell 100 copies a day
- Sell 500 t-shirts a month (I've seen this happen!)
- Flip cars
- Offer a writing service
- Create a piece of software and sell it
- Look for a sales job where I get paid on commissions
- Fill out 5000 surveys a month (they're only worth a dollar?)

- Find a generous person to take pity on me
- Sell everything I own and reinvest the profits into lottery tickets
- Recycle scrap metal
- Buy a few homes and rent them out

As you can see, the ideas are varied. That's the point. It is all about letting your brain expand, think out of the box, and come up with potential ideas before we get to the next step. I also want to point out that I know some of these numbers might sound huge to you. $5k/month can sound crazy-unattainable. But all of these things are possible – and more. I've seen these things happen time and time again when people stretch their minds.

Step #3: Break it down, so it all happens on your terms.

Now we're going to use that big list and use the process of elimination to cross off what you don't want to do. The intention is for you to feel pumped, happy, alive, enriched during the process, so as you're going through your list, keep in mind the feelings you'd like to feel when you're working towards, and achieving your goals. Cross out anything that contradicts those feelings.

For example, if your favorite feeling is "pride," you probably would not want to find a rich person to take pity on you. If your favorite feeling is "secure," you might not want a commission based job.

You'll also want to cross out anything that seems completely unrealistic but be careful, as what you've been thinking of as 'realistic' hasn't got you where you wanted to go...so think twice before crossing something or doesn't seem to fit at all in your personality or skill set (keeping in mind that you can learn new skills – but don't choose, say, coaching, if you hate having a schedule), that you're totally turned off by, or that just doesn't seem anywhere as significant as other options.

48

We're going to narrow this down to the best business model for you. So go through your list again and look for what fits in most with your desired feelings, what works best for your skill set, what excites you the most, what you have the most to offer with, and what you feel the most comfortable with.

If you're not sure how much a action step fits in with your personal feelings, consider how you'll feel as you do certain activities. Will you feel excited? Joyful? Happy? After you whittle down, you may end up having a few options to choose from. And that's ok! The reality is, it's possible that you could take one of MANY routes and still end up achieving your desired result.

So, if you have a list of a few things that fit in with the feelings you want to feel and your skill set, just decide. Use your gut as the tie breaker. For example, here, let's say that we decide we want to have a membership site where we have 250 people pay us $20 a month. Now we can move on to the next step.

I know this planning stuff might not be a barrel of fun at this moment but keep at it. You're going to thank yourself so much later as you gain clarity and get your feet firmly planted on the right path for yourself.

Step #4: Start mapping it out.

So in my example, we know we want to create a membership site where 250 people are paying us $20. Because I'm used to working on the internet, this feels good to me. Don't worry if this is unfamiliar to you – it's just an example and will help illustrate the detail you need to create and ACHIEVE incredible goals that are perfect for you! Now we need to figure out HOW to make this happen.

We're just going to break it down. What needs to happen to have a membership site? Don't get overwhelmed here. Getting everything listed out is extremely helpful in understanding what we need to plan out for the future.

Your initial list might look like this (we'll get into the 'how' of these steps further below):

1. Pick a market that you want to serve. (Or maybe you already know.)
2. Talk to people in the market. See what their frustrations are and figure out a way you
   can genuinely help them and create something they'd love to pay for.
3. Create what people said they wanted to pay for.
4. Get a website.
5. Create sales material for the site.
6. Add in a way where people can pay you.
7. Get the select pieces taken care of.
8. Get members to pay you.

Now, as you do this, you might be thinking "OMG! It sounds outrageously stressful! It looks like I'll never have fun for the rest of my life!" GOOD! Honor that thought. Don't block it out because you should be "thinking positive," don't tell yourself that you're sabotaging yourself or that you're lazy or do anything where you don't honor the real doubts you have. We're going to listen to the voices in your head and find solutions for what they're legitimately concerned about.

See, our minds are very powerful. And when you ask yourself the right questions, you'll be amazed at the answers that you come up with. You can use your objections to finding impressive solutions. Let me show you.

If you're worried that you're not going to have any fun while creating a membership site – especially if you're new at this, ask yourself: "How can I get all of this done in a way that still feels fun?" Your mind might come up with all kinds of answers, like: Make sure that I take an hour to do a fun activity every single day. Make it a game to get things done quickly.

Find other people who are doing this too so you can have a support team. Come up with fun rewards for myself as you hit certain milestones. And on and on and on. You may also be worried that all of this is going to be too overwhelming for you. So trust your brain and ask yourself, "How can I do this in a way that doesn't make me feel overwhelmed?" Some answers you might come up with:

Break it down so that I only need to do 1-3 tasks per day.
 · Hire a coach to help walk me through what I need to do.
 · Outsource tasks I don't understand.
 · Take deep breaths frequently.
 · Start a yoga practice.
 · And on and on and on.

2. Seeing Opportunities

Keys To Actually Making All Of This Happen. Now you have a simple structure on how to map out your goals and get them into tangible action plans. And while that alone might work for some people, I think there are a few elements to consider to make sure you get the most from this book. The next few sections are all about how you can maximize your goal setting and start to drive home results you can be proud of.

So let's get going.

3. Creating the Perfect Daily To-Do Lists

When you start to create your daily action plans, it can be very easy to over-tax yourself or stress yourself out. That's why I'm giving you 3 of my best-of-the-best tips to create your perfect to-do list:

1. Your to-do lists should have no more than 1-5 items.

If you have a list with more than that, it's highly likely that while you may have momentum, in the beginning, you'll end up burning yourself out over the long-term. Maybe in the outset, when you're super-excited, you can ride the momentum. But as soon as you start to feel yourself get tired, STOP. With productivity, less can be a lot more - especially when you plan correctly from the beginning. Don't burn yourself out.

Also, if you have zillion things on your list as many people do, the odds are that you can't get them done. I think that starts to chip away at your personal integrity after a while. You start to see yourself as a person who can't get everything done. It doesn't feel right. Besides that, a lot of times, big to-do lists are just creating busy work for yourself.

2. Start with your hardest items first.

Do your most challenging work first because it's when you're the freshest and most alert. Also, it's very easy to put off the more difficult things if they're last on your to-do list. Things suddenly start to "come up" and get in the way. If you can knock out the hardest thing first, doing the other things on your to-do list will be a lot easier. You'll also feel better about what you got done by the time you go to sleep every night.

3. Remember to take small actions consistently.

We live in a very "instant gratification" culture, but the reality is, you can take minuscule actions every day and have them build up over time. You don't have to push hard. When you take that consistent action, day after day, things start to pile up, and real results start to get created.

4. Have Measurable Checkpoints

As you reverse engineer your goals, make sure that you have specific markers along the way that help you make sure you're heading in the right direction. For example, if your plan was to lose 20 pounds in 3 months, then you should know how much you want to lose after month 1, month 2, and month 3. Weighing in at the end of each month will help you see if you're hitting your targets.

If you said you were going to have 20 members by July, make sure your work focus is 100% on getting to that goal. And if, for some reason at the end of the month you haven't been able to get there, then check in to see why not. Start course correcting.

The point of having measurable marker posts throughout your goal timeline is to make sure that you don't end up very far from where you want to be and that you have a dynamic system of checking in throughout your goal period.

5. Keeping a Positive Attitude

As you're going through your lists, there will invariably be setbacks that test you. You might have tech problems, people might not get back to you when they say they will, and things might take much longer than you anticipated that they would. That's all totally OK. The only thing that matters, in any of these setbacks, is how you choose to respond to them.

One empowering outlook is to view obstacles as a test to see how badly you want something. And if you've gone through the goal process, hopefully, you've set yourself up with a strong "why" - and you're not going to let any obstacle deter you. When things happen, I recommend being a "yes" to them. And by that, I mean, instead of fighting them, just acknowledge what's going on. Accept it, and then look for solutions. Fighting things or falling into victim mode is a waste of time. :) Just keep active, feel a certainty that you're going to reach your goals, and don't derail your focus.

6. Get Help

As you're working on your goals, it might benefit you to get some help. Some good times to look into getting help are:
   -Is this the first time you're learning something?
   -Would it benefit you to get instruction from someone who knows the ropes?
   -Are you not sure how to reach your goal? For example - are you struggling with losing
   weight, even though you think you're doing the right things?
   -Are you having a tough time writing your book?

-Is it tough for you to learn to play the piano?

-Are you dreading getting things done because you have no idea what to do next?

In any of these cases, it might be treasured to seek assistance, so you can keep your momentum instead of getting bogged down or overwhelmed by trying to learn everything on your own. Trust me, I know from experience.

7. Make Choices Based On Your Goals

One of the benefits of figuring out what you want and working backward is that it helps you keep focused. As you're working on your plans, and you see bright shiny objects, make sure to reference those objects against your goals. For example, if you're working on a diet plan, and then you hear about a new diet plan come up that looks amazing, remember that you're already working on something. You don't need to be derailed.

Or if you're at a restaurant, and you're offered chocolate cake, think about what your plans are. Occasionally, a piece of chocolate cake might be okay. But remember to turn down temptation too, or else you'll never reach the outcome you're looking for. And remember your desired feelings: e.g. happiness about meeting your ideals, being the healthy person you want to be, etc.

If you're working on a business model and then you see a new business model come your way, remember that you have a thoughtfully considered plan already created and that you don't need to follow whatever looks good. Keep your eyes on the long-term prize. And remember: the people who succeed are those who take focused action.

8. Accountability

One of the best things you can do is have a means of keeping yourself held accountable for your goals. When you have someone (or multiple people) watching you, it can give you that extra push to get things done on days when you'd rather crawl into bed.

There are lots of reasons why people can benefit from accountability, and they vary from person to person. Here are a few of the major reasons to make sure you hold yourself accountable:

-When you set a goal, you don't want to look bad by not reaching it (or at least making

major progress towards it).

-It feels great to know someone is cheering you on. Subconsciously, it's very powerful

just to speak your goals to someone outside of yourself.

There are many ways you can help keep yourself accountable. You can do one or multiple of these at the same time. Work with a friend: You may want to consider getting an accountability partner or even creating a mastermind group full of like-minded people who want to reach the same goals you. Tell the people your goals for each week (or month). And then check in and let people know if you've done what you committed to.

II

Win On Purpose - A 30 Day Journey

I believe that we all hold the secret to our passion and purpose within ourselves. It all comes back to de-cluttering our minds of lots of learned junk that keeps us lost and opening ourselves up to the spark within us that is waiting to break free.

The 30-Day journal prompts will begin triggering some key passion indicators within yourself.

Remember, no matter what emotions arise (fear, judgement, regret etc), be as honest with yourself as you can be. Most importantly, have fun!

10

30-Day Journal Prompts

D^{ay 1}

What are your 3 favorite topics to discuss? What could you talk about for hours on end?

Day 2

When you connect with your heart, what things in life really make you feel free?

Day 3

**What would 5 people who know you best tell you that you
would be amazing at doing ...**

_____

_____

_____

_____

_____

_____

Day 4

**What are your talents? What naturally flows for you without
you even having to try?**

_____

_____

_____

_____

_____

_____

Day 5

**5 people that inspire you... who are they and what is it about
them that inspires you?**

_____

_____

_____

_____

_____

_____

Day 6

If you were to wake up tomorrow feeling truly free and happily excited about your working day ahead, what job would you be doing?

Day 7

You inherit $300 million, how would it change your life? What would you do with the money and your days?

Day 8

You are totally 'in your element' and time seems to have disappeared. What are you doing?

Day 9

What difference do you want to make in the world?

_____

_____

_____

_____

_____

_____

Day 10

A genie has granted you the wish that whichever career you choose will not fail. Which do you choose?

_____

_____

_____

_____

_____

_____

Day 11

It is your birthday and somebody buys you an annual magazine subscription. Which type would you love it to be and Why?

_____

_____

_____

_____

_____

_____

Day 12

What fundamental beliefs do you feel truly passionate about?

Day 13

Intrinsically, do you feel as though you were actually born to do a particular thing? Why?

Day 14

If you could blindly believe that you would make money from your creativity, what would you be doing ?

Day 15

When you are dead and gone, what would you like people to say about the way you lived your life?

_____
_____
_____

Day 16
What areas of life are you naturally drawn to?

_____
_____
_____
_____
_____
_____

Day 17
What do people ask you for information/advice about?

_____
_____
_____
_____
_____
_____

Day 18
What careers do you have wild dreams of having?

_____
_____
_____
_____
_____
_____

Day 19

If you were to pioneer a cause around the world, and it was guaranteed to be a success, what would it be?

_____

_____

_____

_____

_____

_____

Day 20

What do you love to do when you have free time and what is it that gives you that real buzz of excitement?

_____

_____

_____

_____

_____

_____

Day 21

What topics interest you and what would you really love to know lots more about?

_____

_____

_____

_____

_____

_____

Day 22

If someone were to pay all of your living costs and expenses for

2 years, what work would you pursue in that time?

Day 23

When you were a child, what did you always dream of doing when you got older?
What do they symbolize?

Day 24

If you were to change 3 things in the world for the greater good, what would they be?

Day 25

What is it that you would regret not doing with your life, if you were to die tomorrow?

Day 26

You love helping people with these 3 different things. What are they?

Day 27

A successful entrepreneur teaches you for 3 years how to make money from 1 area of your choice, all for free. What do you choose & Why?

Day 28

What piece of knowledge do you feel as though you would love to share with the world?

_____
_____
_____

Day 29

**The person that loves you most in the whole world asks you
what you need to be doing with your life to be really happy.
How do you respond?**

_____
_____
_____
_____
_____
_____

Day 30

If you had 5 years left to live, what would you do?

_____
_____
_____
_____
_____
_____

About the Author

Shanae Starnes, BBA, MA Ed. known as the Inspirational Motivator is an Author, Financial Literacy Consultant, Entrepreneur, Mother, and Cosmetology Career and Technical educator living her dreams. Shanae is a self-starter, who has taken every opportunity to strengthen her background. Her peers and colleagues describe her as a compassionate leader who is committed to empowering others.

With over twenty years of knowledge and training in cosmetology, public speaking, a strong background in customer relations, and a genuine desire to help others love themselves; Shanae Starnes is truly an example of what it means to live your dreams. For more information email starnesshanae@gmail.com.

The Co-Author of H.E.R. Extreme Makeover: Reflections of Healing, Equipping and Restoring Life's Messes Into Masterpieces, a story about resilience and faith and The Purposed Woman: 365 Day Devotional books. In her book, *Keeping Score* Shanae shows and encourages others how to better handle their credit which in turn helps people improve their finances. Manifesting one's financial literacy has been her focus now since 2013 when she began her tax preparation business

Ideal Tax and Bookkeeping Inc. Her company also assist with creating budgets, credit education/restoration, asset protection through health & life insurance and financial literacy.

You can connect with me on:

- https://shanaestarnes.blog
- https://twitter.com/Shanaedastylist
- https://www.facebook.com/dawnshanae

www.ingramcontent.com/pod-product-compliance
Lightning Source LLC
LaVergne TN
LVHW052037080426
835513LV00018B/2368